Publications International, Ltd.

Pictured on the front cover *(clockwise from top)*: Strawberry Snow Cones *(page 100)*, JELL-O Firecrackers *(page 78)*, Chocolate-Peanut Butter Cupcakes *(page 110)* and Chocolate Elf Bites *(page 80)*.

Pictured on the back cover *(from left to right)*: Mini "Mimosas" *(page 26)*, Melon Bubbles *(page 14)*, and Black Forest Cupcakes *(page 120)*.

ISBN: 978-1-4508-8457-0

Library of Congress Control Number: 2013954580

Manufactured in China.

8 7 6 5 4 3 2 1

Microwave Cooking: Microwave ovens vary in wattage. Use the cooking times as guidelines and check for doneness before adding more time.

Preparation/Cooking Times: Preparation times are based on the approximate amount of time required to assemble the recipe before cooking, baking, chilling, or serving. These times include preparation steps such as measuring, chopping, and mixing. The fact that some preparations and cooking can be done simultaneously is taken into account. Preparation of optional ingredients and serving suggestions is not included.

Publications International, Ltd.

contents

quick & easy desserts

Stress-free sweets with little prep or bake time

triple-chocolate cookie balls

PREP: 30 min. | TOTAL: 1 hour 10 min. | MAKES: 42 servings.

▸ what you need!

½ cup cold milk

1 pkg. (3.9 oz.) JELL-O Chocolate Instant Pudding

36 chocolate sandwich cookies, finely crushed (about 3 cups)

3 pkg. (4 oz. each) BAKER'S Semi-Sweet Chocolate (12 oz.), broken into pieces, melted

1 oz. BAKER'S White Chocolate, melted

▸ make it!

STIR milk and dry pudding mix in medium bowl with large spoon just until pudding mix is moistened. Immediately stir in cookie crumbs; mix well.

SHAPE into 42 (1-inch) balls. Freeze 10 min. Dip in semi-sweet chocolate; place in single layer in shallow waxed paper-lined pan.

REFRIGERATE 20 min. or until firm. Drizzle with white chocolate; refrigerate 10 min. or until firm.

SIZE-WISE:
Enjoy your favorite foods on occasion but remember to keep tabs on portions.

SPECIAL EXTRA:
Use a food processor to finely crush the cookies, and use a mini cookie dough scoop to make uniformly sized cookie balls.

"sangria" fruit cups

PREP: 20 min. | TOTAL: 4 hours 20 min. | MAKES: 8 servings, about ½ cup each.

▸ what you need!

1 cup orange juice

1 pkg. (3 oz.) JELL-O Strawberry Flavor Gelatin

1 pkg. (3 oz.) JELL-O Lemon Flavor Gelatin

1½ cups cold water

1 cup pitted fresh sweet cherries, halved

8 strawberries, quartered

1 nectarine, peeled and sliced

1 cup thawed COOL WHIP Whipped Topping

▸ make it!

BRING orange juice to boil. Add to dry gelatin mixes in medium bowl; stir 2 min. until completely dissolved. Stir in cold water.

SPOON fruit into 8 clear cups. Cover with gelatin mixture.

REFRIGERATE 4 hours or until firm. Top with COOL WHIP just before serving.

cherry celebration

▶ what you need!

2 cups boiling water

2 pkg. (3 oz. each) JELL-O Cherry Flavor Gelatin

4 cups ice cubes

3 cups thawed COOL WHIP Whipped Topping

1 cup cherry pie filling

▶ make it!

STIR boiling water into dry gelatin mixes in large bowl until completely dissolved. Add ice; stir until gelatin starts to thicken. Remove any unmelted ice.

ADD COOL WHIP; stir with wire whisk until blended. Refrigerate 20 min. or until slightly thickened.

STIR in pie filling; spoon into 12 champagne glasses or glass bowl. Refrigerate 4 hours or until firm. Garnish with additional COOL WHIP and cherry pie filling just before serving, if desired.

cappuccino dessert

PREP: 10 min. | TOTAL: 1 hour 10 min. | MAKES: 5 servings.

▶ what you need!

1 pkg. (1 oz.) JELL-O Vanilla Flavor Fat Free Sugar Free Instant Pudding

2 tsp. MAXWELL HOUSE Instant Coffee

2 cups cold fat-free milk

⅛ tsp. ground cinnamon

1 cup thawed COOL WHIP LITE Whipped Topping

▶ make it!

BEAT dry pudding mix, coffee granules and milk with whisk 2 min.; pour into 5 dessert dishes.

REFRIGERATE 1 hour.

STIR cinnamon into COOL WHIP with whisk. Spoon over pudding.

beautifully easy fruit tart

PREP: 15 min. | TOTAL: 45 min. | MAKES: 9 servings.

▶ what you need!

1 sheet frozen puff pastry (½ of 17.3-oz. pkg.), thawed

1 pkg. (3.4 oz.) JELL-O Vanilla Flavor Instant Pudding

1 cup cold milk

1 cup thawed COOL WHIP Whipped Topping

1 oz. BAKER'S White Chocolate

1 cup quartered fresh strawberries

1 can (11 oz.) mandarin oranges, drained

1 kiwi, peeled, sliced and halved

3 Tbsp. apricot preserves

2 tsp. water

▶ make it!

HEAT oven to 400°F.

UNROLL pastry on baking sheet. Fold over edges of pastry to form ½-inch rim; press together firmly to seal. Prick pastry sheet with fork. Bake 10 to 15 min. or until puffed and golden brown. Cool completely. Place on tray.

BEAT dry pudding mix and milk in large bowl with whisk 2 min. Stir in COOL WHIP; spread onto pastry.

MELT chocolate as directed on package. Arrange fruit over pudding mixture. Mix preserves and water; brush onto fruit. Drizzle with chocolate. Let stand until chocolate is firm.

melon bubbles

PREP: 15 min. | TOTAL: 4 hours 45 min. | MAKES: 8 servings.

▸ what you need!

1½ cups boiling water

2 pkg. (3 oz. each) JELL-O Melon Fusion Flavor Gelatin

2½ cups cold club soda

⅓ cup each: cantaloupe, honeydew and watermelon balls

▸ make it!

STIR boiling water into dry gelatin mixes in large bowl at least 2 min. until completely dissolved. Stir in club soda. Refrigerate 1½ hours or until thickened (spoon drawn through leaves definite impression).

MEASURE 1 cup thickened gelatin into medium bowl; set aside. Stir melon balls into remaining gelatin. Spoon into 8 martini or dessert glasses.

BEAT reserved gelatin with electric mixer on high speed until fluffy and about doubled in volume. Spoon over gelatin in glasses. Refrigerate 3 hours or until firm. Store leftovers in refrigerator.

creamy layered squares

PREP: 15 min. | TOTAL: 4 hours | MAKES: 9 servings, 1 square each.

▸ what you need!

1½ cups boiling water

1 pkg. (0.6 oz.) JELL-O Strawberry Flavor Sugar Free Gelatin

Ice cubes

1 cup cold water

1½ cups thawed COOL WHIP Sugar Free Whipped Topping, divided

▸ make it!

ADD boiling water to dry gelatin mix in large bowl; stir 2 min. until completely dissolved. Add enough ice to cold water to measure 1½ cups. Add to gelatin; stir until ice is completely melted. Remove 1½ cups gelatin; set aside on counter. Refrigerate remaining gelatin 30 min. or until slightly thickened.

ADD ¾ cup of the COOL WHIP to chilled, thickened gelatin; stir with wire whisk until well blended. Pour into 8-inch square dish. Refrigerate 15 min. or until gelatin mixture is set but not firm. Carefully pour reserved gelatin over creamy layer in dish.

REFRIGERATE 3 hours or until firm. Cut into squares; top with remaining COOL WHIP.

delightful lemon mousse
with raspberry sauce

PREP: 15 min. | TOTAL: 4 hours 15 min. | MAKES: 10 servings.

▸ what you need!

1½ cups boiling water

1 pkg. (0.3 oz.) JELL-O Lemon Flavor Sugar Free Gelatin

2 tsp. grated lemon zest

Ice cubes

1 cup cold apple juice

1 tub (8 oz.) COOL WHIP FREE Whipped Topping, thawed

1 pkg. (10 oz.) frozen raspberries or strawberries, thawed, puréed in blender

▸ make it!

STIR boiling water into dry gelatin mix and lemon zest in large bowl at least 2 min. until completely dissolved. Add enough ice to apple juice to measure 1¾ cups. Stir into gelatin until slightly thickened.

STIR in COOL WHIP with whisk until well blended. Pour half the raspberry sauce into 10 dessert dishes. Top with gelatin mixture and remaining raspberry sauce.

REFRIGERATE 4 hours or until firm. Store any leftover dessert in refrigerator.

chocolate-peanut butter bonbons

PREP: 20 min. | TOTAL: 2 hours 20 min. | MAKES: 24 servings.

▶ what you need!

4 oz. (½ of 8-oz. pkg.) PHILADELPHIA Cream Cheese, softened

¾ cup milk

1 pkg. (3.9 oz.) JELL-O Chocolate Instant Pudding

1 cup thawed COOL WHIP Whipped Topping

24 vanilla wafers

1 tub (7 oz.) BAKER'S Milk Chocolate Dipping Chocolate

2 Tbsp. PLANTERS Creamy Peanut Butter

½ cup PLANTERS COCKTAIL Peanuts, chopped

▶ make it!

BEAT cream cheese in large bowl with mixer until creamy. Gradually beat in milk. Add dry pudding mix; beat 2 min. Whisk in COOL WHIP.

SPOON into resealable plastic bag; cut small corner from bottom of bag. Pipe about 1 Tbsp. pudding mixture into each of 24 paper-lined mini muffin cups; stand wafer in each cup. Freeze 2 hours or until firm.

PEEL liners off bonbons. Melt dipping chocolate as directed on package; stir in peanut butter until melted. Dip bottom halves of bonbons in chocolate, then in nuts. Place on waxed paper-covered baking sheet. Let stand until chocolate is firm.

SIZE-WISE:
These bonbons are mini treats featuring built-in portion control. Enjoy one when you want something sweet.

MAKE AHEAD:
Bonbons can be stored in freezer up to 2 days before dipping in chocolate and nuts as directed. Dipped bonbons can be stored in freezer up to 1 month before serving.

NOTE:
If you don't have a mini muffin pan, place paper mini muffin cups on baking sheet before filling as directed.

black and white pudding squares

PREP: 20 min. | TOTAL: 4 hours 20 min. | MAKES: 24 servings.

▶ what you need!

24 chocolate sandwich cookies, finely crushed (about 2 cups)

¼ cup butter, melted

1 pkg. (8 oz.) PHILADELPHIA Cream Cheese, softened

2 pkg. (3.4 oz. each) JELL-O Vanilla Flavor Instant Pudding

3 cups cold milk, divided

1 pkg. (3.9 oz.) JELL-O Chocolate Instant Pudding

▶ make it!

MIX first 2 ingredients; press onto bottom of 13×9-inch pan.

BEAT cream cheese, dry vanilla pudding mixes and 1½ cups milk in large bowl with mixer until well blended; spread over crust.

BEAT chocolate pudding mix and remaining milk with whisk 2 min.; spoon into resealable plastic food storage bag. Snip off small corner from bottom of bag. Inserting tip into pudding mixture, squeeze chocolate pudding into 6 lengthwise stripes over vanilla pudding. Drag toothpick through the stripes to decorate. Refrigerate 4 hours.

HOW TO EASILY SERVE DESSERT:
Line pan with plastic wrap, with ends of wrap extending over sides. Freeze 2 hours. Let stand 10 min. Use plastic wrap handles to lift dessert from pan before cutting.

VARIATION:
Prepare as directed, except use 2 pkg. chocolate pudding and 1 pkg. vanilla pudding. Use the chocolate pudding to prepare the cream cheese-pudding base, then swirl the vanilla pudding into the chocolate base.

chocolate-cherry bombs

PREP: 15 min. | TOTAL: 45 min. | MAKES: 14 servings.

▶ what you need!

⅓ cup boiling water

1 pkg. (3 oz.) JELL-O Cherry Flavor Gelatin

1 can (5 oz.) evaporated milk

2 oz. BAKER'S Semi-Sweet Chocolate, coarsely chopped

14 maraschino cherries with stems, drained

▶ make it!

ADD boiling water to dry gelatin mix in medium bowl; stir 2 min. until completely dissolved.

MICROWAVE evaporated milk and chocolate in microwaveable bowl on HIGH 2 min. or until chocolate is melted and mixture is blended, stirring each minute. Add to gelatin; whisk until blended.

POUR into 14 (3 oz.) paper cups sprayed with cooking spray. Refrigerate 15 min.

TOP with cherries, pressing in slightly to stick. Refrigerate 20 min. or until firm. Unmold to serve.

VARIATION:
Substitute mini muffin pan or ice cube tray for paper cups.

SUBSTITUTE:
Prepare using 1 pkg. (0.3 oz.) JELL-O Cherry Flavor Sugar Free Gelatin.

mini "mimosas"

PREP: 10 min. | TOTAL: 1 hour 20 min. | MAKES: 10 servings.

▶ what you need!

¼ cup boiling water

1 pkg. (3 oz.) JELL-O Orange Flavor Gelatin

⅓ cup cold club soda

2 fresh strawberries, each cut crosswise into 5 slices

▶ make it!

ADD boiling water to dry gelatin mix in small bowl; stir 2 min. until completely dissolved. Stir in club soda.

PLACE strawberries in 10 (2-oz.) plastic cups sprayed with cooking spray; fill with gelatin. Refrigerate 1 hour or until firm.

UNMOLD before serving.

SUBSTITUTE:
Prepare using JELL-O Sugar Free Gelatin.

SUBSTITUTE:
Substitute boiling orange juice for the boiling water.

VARIATION:
Cut each strawberry into 5 wedges instead of slicing it. Prepare gelatin mixture as directed; pour into 2-oz. plastic cups sprayed with cooking spray. Refrigerate 10 min. Insert strawberry wedge into gelatin in each cup. Refrigerate 1 hour or until firm.

strawberry 'n cream minis

PREP: 15 min. | TOTAL: 45 min. | MAKES: 14 servings.

▶ what you need!

⅓ cup boiling water

1 pkg. (3 oz.) JELL-O Strawberry Flavor Gelatin

1 can (5 oz.) evaporated milk

2 oz. BAKER'S White Chocolate

4 fresh strawberries, quartered

▶ make it!

ADD boiling water to dry gelatin mix in medium bowl; stir 2 min. until completely dissolved.

MICROWAVE evaporated milk and chocolate in microwaveable bowl on HIGH 2 min. or until chocolate is completely melted and mixture is well blended, stirring after each minute. Add to gelatin; beat with mixer until well blended.

SPOON into 14 sections of ice cube trays sprayed with cooking spray. Refrigerate 20 min. or until firm.

UNMOLD gelatin cubes just before serving; top with berries.

SUBSTITUTE:
Prepare using 1 pkg. (0.3 oz.) JELL-O Strawberry Flavor Sugar Free Gelatin.

VARIATION:
Refrigerate gelatin mixture in 9×5-inch loaf pan instead of in the ice cube trays. Unmold gelatin mixture, then cut into 16 rectangles. Serve topped with strawberries. Makes 16 servings.

confetti fudge bites

PREP: 15 min. | TOTAL: 2 hours 15 min. | MAKES: 24 servings.

▸ what you need!

1½ pkg. (4 oz. each) BAKER'S White Chocolate (6 oz.)

6 Tbsp. butter or margarine

⅓ cup water

1 pkg. (3.4 oz.) JELL-O Vanilla Flavor Instant Pudding

3 cups powdered sugar

6 Tbsp. multi-colored sprinkles, divided

▸ make it!

LINE 8-inch square pan with foil, with ends of foil extending over sides. Microwave chocolate, butter and water in large microwaveable bowl on HIGH 2 min. or until butter is melted; stir until chocolate is completely melted. Add dry pudding mix; stir with whisk 2 min.

ADD powdered sugar, 1 cup at a time, stirring after each addition until blended. Stir in ¼ cup sprinkles; press onto bottom of prepared pan. Top with remaining sprinkles.

REFRIGERATE 2 hours or until firm.

STORAGE KNOW-HOW:
Store cut-up fudge between sheets of waxed paper in airtight container in refrigerator up to 2 weeks.

mosaic dessert bars

PREP: 20 min. | TOTAL: 4 hours 20 min. | MAKES: 16 servings.

▸ what you need!

5½ cups boiling water, divided

1 pkg. (3 oz.) JELL-O Strawberry Flavor Gelatin

1 pkg. (3 oz.) JELL-O Lime Flavor Gelatin

1 pkg. (3 oz.) JELL-O Orange Flavor Gelatin

1 pkg. (3 oz.) JELL-O Lemon Flavor Gelatin

2 env. KNOX* Unflavored Gelatine

½ cup cold water

1 can (14 oz.) sweetened condensed milk

▸ make it!

ADD 1 cup boiling water to each flavor fruit gelatin mix in separate bowls; stir 2 min. until completely dissolved. Pour each flavor of gelatin into separate small shallow food storage container sprayed with cooking spray. Refrigerate 2 hours or until firm.

SPRINKLE unflavored gelatine over cold water; let stand 1 min. Stir in remaining boiling water. Add condensed milk; mix well. Cool slightly.

CUT flavored gelatin into cubes. Randomly place cubes in 13×9-inch pan sprayed with cooking spray. Pour milk mixture over cubes; stir to evenly distribute gelatin cubes. Refrigerate 2 hours or until firm before cutting into bars.

VARIATION:
Prepare recipe in 9×5-inch loaf pan. Unmold, then slice to serve.

KNOX is a registered trademark of Kraft Foods Global, Inc.

kid favorites

Desserts kids love to make and eat

easy pudding cookies

PREP: 15 min. | TOTAL: 27 min. | MAKES: about 3½ dozen or 42 servings, 1 cookie each.

▶ what you need!

- 1 cup butter or margarine, softened
- 1 cup packed brown sugar
- 1 pkg. (3.9 oz.) JELL-O Chocolate Instant Pudding
- 2 eggs
- 1 tsp. baking soda
- 2 cups flour
- 1½ pkg. (4 oz. each) BAKER'S White Chocolate (6 oz.), chopped

▶ make it!

HEAT oven to 350°F.

BEAT butter and sugar in large bowl with mixer until light and fluffy. Add dry pudding mix; beat until blended. Add eggs and baking soda; mix well. Gradually add flour, beating after each addition until well blended. Stir in chocolate.

DROP tablespoonfuls of dough, 2 inches apart, onto baking sheets.

BAKE 10 to 12 min. or until edges are lightly browned. Cool 1 min. on baking sheets; remove to wire racks. Cool completely.

rocky road cups

PREP: 10 min. | TOTAL: 1 hour 10 min. | MAKES: 12 servings.

▶ what you need!

2 cups cold milk

2 pkg. (3.9 oz. each) JELL-O Chocolate Flavor Instant Pudding

2 cups thawed COOL WHIP Whipped Topping

1 cup PLANTERS COCKTAIL Peanuts

1 pkg. (4 oz.) BAKER'S Semi-Sweet Chocolate, chopped

1 cup JET-PUFFED Miniature Marshmallows

▶ make it!

POUR milk into large bowl. Add dry pudding mixes. Beat with wire whisk 2 min. or until well blended. Gently stir in COOL WHIP.

ADD remaining ingredients; stir gently until well blended. Spoon evenly into 12 dessert dishes or cups.

REFRIGERATE at least 1 hour before serving. Store leftover desserts in refrigerator.

chocolate holiday bears

PREP: 20 min. | TOTAL: 49 min. | MAKES: 20 servings.

▶ what you need!

¾ cup butter or margarine, softened

¾ cup packed brown sugar

1 pkg. (3.9 oz.) JELL-O Chocolate Instant Pudding

1 egg

1¾ cups flour

1 tsp. baking soda

3 oz. BAKER'S Semi-Sweet Chocolate

Decorations: assorted small candies, raisins, sprinkles, JET-PUFFED Miniature Marshmallows, colored sugars or licorice strips

▶ make it!

HEAT oven to 350°F.

BEAT first 4 ingredients with mixer until well blended. Mix flour and baking soda; gradually add to pudding mixture, beating until well blended after each addition. Shape into ball.

ROLL out dough on lightly floured surface to ¼-inch thickness. Cut out dough using 4-inch bear-shaped cookie cutter; place, 2 inches apart, on greased baking sheets. Reroll scraps and use to cut additional cookies.

BAKE 12 to 14 min. or until slightly firm. Let stand on baking sheets 2 min.; remove to wire racks. Cool completely.

MELT chocolate; spread on bottom half of bears for pants or skirts. Decorate with small candies, raisins, sprinkles or marshmallows for eyes, mouth and buttons, pressing decorations lightly into dough to secure. Use remaining chocolate to attach remaining decorations. Let stand until chocolate is firm.

sweetheart chocolate pizza

PREP: 20 min. | TOTAL: 1 hour | MAKES: 12 servings.

▶ what you need!

- 5 oz. BAKER'S Semi-Sweet Chocolate, divided
- 1 pkg. (16.5 oz.) refrigerated sugar cookie dough
- 1 pkg. (3.9 oz.) JELL-O Chocolate Instant Pudding
- 1 cup cold milk
- ¼ cup powdered sugar
- 1 tub (8 oz.) COOL WHIP Whipped Topping, thawed, divided
- 1½ cups halved strawberries

▶ make it!

HEAT oven to 375°F.

MICROWAVE 4 oz. chocolate in medium microwaveable bowl as directed on package. Add cookie dough; mix well. Press onto bottom of 12-inch pizza pan. Bake 10 min. Cool completely.

BEAT dry pudding mix and milk in separate medium bowl with whisk 2 min. Stir in sugar. Add half the COOL WHIP; mix well. Spread onto crust.

SPREAD remaining COOL WHIP in heart shape over pudding. Decorate with berries. Melt remaining chocolate; drizzle evenly over dessert. Let stand until chocolate is firm. Cut into wedges to serve.

snowman cups

PREP: 15 min. | TOTAL: 15 min. | MAKES: 10 servings, ½ cup each.

▸ what you need!

    2 pkg. (3.9 oz. each) JELL-O Chocolate Instant Pudding

    1 qt. (4 cups) cold milk

   20 chocolate sandwich cookies, crushed (about 2 cups), divided

    2 cups thawed COOL WHIP Whipped Topping

      Assorted decorating gels

▸ make it!

BEAT dry pudding mixes and milk with whisk 2 min. Let stand 5 min. Stir in 1 cup cookie crumbs.

SPOON remaining cookie crumbs into 10 (6- to 7-oz.) plastic cups; cover with pudding mixture.

DROP spoonfuls of COOL WHIP onto desserts to resemble snowmen. Decorate with gels as shown in photo.

JELL-O holiday JIGGLERS

PREP: 10 min. | TOTAL: 3 hours 10 min. | MAKES: 2 dozen or 24 servings, 1 JIGGLERS each.

▶ what you need!

2½ cups boiling water

4 pkg. (3 oz. each) JELL-O Gelatin, any red flavor

▶ make it!

ADD boiling water to dry gelatin mixes; stir 3 min. until completely dissolved.

POUR into 13×9-inch pan. Refrigerate 3 hours or until firm.

DIP bottom of pan in warm water 15 sec. Cut gelatin into shapes using JELL-O Holiday JIGGLERS Cutters.

VARIATION:

Prepare using 2 different colors of gelatin. For each color, use 2 pkg. gelatin, 1¼ cups boiling water and an 8- or 9-inch square pan.

JELL-O "dive-on-in" cake

PREP: 20 min. | TOTAL: 4 hours 25 min. | MAKES: 20 servings, 1 piece each.

▶ what you need!

- 1 pkg. (2-layer size) yellow cake mix
- 2 cups boiling water
- 2 pkg. (3 oz. each) JELL-O Berry Blue Flavor Gelatin
- 1 cup cold water
- 1 tub (8 oz.) COOL WHIP Whipped Topping, thawed
- 56 mini chocolate sandwich cookies
- 6 teddy bear-shaped graham snacks
- 5 ring-shaped chewy fruit snacks
- 4 bite-size fish-shaped chewy fruit snacks
- 1 small rectangular graham cracker

▶ make it!

PREPARE and bake cake mix in 13×9-inch baking pan as directed on package. Cool completely. Invert cake onto large platter; remove pan. Using a serrated knife, cut and scoop out a shallow rectangle from center of cake, leaving a 2-inch border of cake on all sides and a thin layer of cake on the bottom. Reserve removed cake for snacking or other use.

STIR boiling water into dry gelatin mixes in large bowl at least 2 min., or until completely dissolved. Stir in cold water. Refrigerate 1¼ hours or until slightly thickened (consistency of unbeaten egg whites). Pour thickened gelatin into center of cake. Refrigerate 3 hours or until set.

FROST borders of cake with COOL WHIP. Decorate with remaining ingredients as desired to resemble a swimming pool. Store leftover cake in refrigerator.

floating fruit parfaits

PREP: 15 min. | TOTAL: 1 hour 35 min. | MAKES: 6 servings.

▶ what you need!

½ cup sliced fresh strawberries

¾ cup boiling water

1 pkg. (0.3 oz.) JELL-O Strawberry Flavor Sugar Free Gelatin

½ cup cold water

¾ cup ice cubes

1 cup plus 6 Tbsp. thawed COOL WHIP LITE Whipped Topping, divided

▶ make it!

SPOON berries into 6 parfait or dessert glasses. Add boiling water to dry gelatin mix in medium bowl; stir 2 min. until completely dissolved. Add cold water and ice cubes; stir until ice is melted. Pour ¾ cup gelatin evenly over berries. Refrigerate 20 min. or until gelatin is set but not firm. Meanwhile let remaining gelatin stand at room temperature until cooled and ready to be used.

ADD 1 cup COOL WHIP to remaining gelatin; stir with whisk until blended. Spoon over gelatin in glasses.

REFRIGERATE 1 hour or until firm. Serve topped with remaining COOL WHIP.

VARIATION:
Prepare using JELL-O Orange Flavor Sugar Free Gelatin and cantaloupe balls for the strawberries.

chocolate-peanut butter candy dessert

▶ what you need!

12 chocolate sandwich cookies, crushed

2 Tbsp. butter, melted

2 cups cold milk

½ cup PLANTERS Creamy Peanut Butter

2 pkg. (3.9 oz. each) JELL-O Chocolate Instant Pudding

2 cups thawed COOL WHIP Whipped Topping, divided

2 Tbsp. hot fudge ice cream topping

¼ cup candy-coated peanut butter pieces

▶ make it!

MIX crushed cookies and butter; press onto bottom of 8-inch square pan.

ADD milk gradually to peanut butter in large bowl, stirring with whisk until well blended. Add dry pudding mixes; beat 2 min. (Mixture will be thick.) Stir in 1 cup COOL WHIP. Spread onto crust; cover with remaining COOL WHIP.

REFRIGERATE 3 hours or until firm. When ready to serve, microwave fudge topping as directed on label; drizzle over dessert. Top with peanut butter pieces.

aquarium cups

PREP: 15 min. | TOTAL: 1 hour 15 min. | MAKES: 4 servings, about ½ cup each.

▶ what you need!

¾ cup boiling water

1 pkg. (3 oz.) JELL-O Berry Blue Flavor Gelatin

Ice cubes

½ cup cold water

½ cup chopped strawberries

4 bite-size fish-shaped chewy fruit snacks

▶ make it!

ADD boiling water to dry gelatin in medium bowl; stir 2 min. until completely dissolved. Add enough ice cubes to cold water to measure 1¼ cups. Add to gelatin; stir until slightly thickened. Remove any unmelted ice. If gelatin is still thin, refrigerate until slightly thickened.

PLACE berries in 4 clear plastic cups; cover with gelatin. Press fruit snacks into gelatin until completely submerged.

REFRIGERATE 1 hour or until firm.

ghosts in the graveyard

PREP: 15 min. | TOTAL: 1 hour 15 min. | MAKES: 18 servings, about ½ cup each.

▶ what you need!

2 pkg. (3.9 oz. each) JELL-O Chocolate Instant Pudding

3 cups cold milk

1 tub (12 oz.) COOL WHIP Whipped Topping, thawed, divided

15 chocolate sandwich cookies, crushed (about 1½ cups)

Decorations: vanilla creme sandwich cookies, decorating gel, candy pumpkins, candy corn pieces, orange jelly beans, mini semi-sweet chocolate chips

▶ make it!

BEAT dry pudding mixes and milk in large bowl with whisk 2 min. Let stand 5 min. Stir in 3 cups COOL WHIP and half of the cookie crumbs. Spread into 13×9-inch dish; sprinkle with remaining crumbs.

REFRIGERATE 1 hour. Meanwhile, decorate creme sandwich cookies with decorating gel to resemble tombstones.

INSERT decorated cookies into top of dessert just before serving. Add candies. Drop large spoonfuls of remaining COOL WHIP onto dessert to resemble ghosts.

chocolate-peanut butter and pretzel bars

PREP: 35 min. | TOTAL: 2 hours 35 min. | MAKES: 24 servings.

▸ what you need!

2 cups finely crushed pretzels

⅔ cup butter, melted

¼ cup sugar

2 pkg. (3.9 oz. each) JELL-O Chocolate Instant Pudding

2 cups cold milk

1 cup PLANTERS Creamy Peanut Butter, divided

1¾ cups thawed COOL WHIP Whipped Topping, divided

2 bananas, sliced

24 miniature pretzel twists

▸ make it!

HEAT oven to 350°F.

MIX first 3 ingredients until well blended; press onto bottom of 13×9-inch pan. Bake 10 min.; cool completely. Meanwhile, beat dry pudding mixes, milk and ¾ cup peanut butter in medium bowl with whisk until well blended. Stir in ¾ cup COOL WHIP.

SPREAD ¾ cup peanut butter mixture over crust; top with bananas and remaining peanut butter mixture.

WHISK remaining peanut butter and half of the remaining COOL WHIP in separate medium bowl until well blended. Stir in remaining COOL WHIP; spread over dessert. Refrigerate 2 hours. Top with whole pretzels just before serving.

NOTE:
You will need to crush about 6 cups miniature pretzel twists to get the 2 cups finely crushed pretzels to make crust.

JAZZ IT UP:
Drizzle pretzels with melted BAKER'S Semi-Sweet Chocolate; let chocolate set. Garnish
dessert with chocolate-covered pretzels.

holiday
celebrations

Simple, stunning creations for every occasion

chocolate-candy cane cupcakes

PREP: 20 min. | TOTAL: 1 hour 23 min. | MAKES: 30 servings.

▸ what you need!

5 oz. BAKER'S Semi-Sweet Chocolate, divided

1 pkg. (2-layer size) chocolate cake mix

1 pkg. (3.9 oz.) JELL-O Chocolate Instant Pudding

1 cup BREAKSTONE'S or KNUDSEN Sour Cream

½ cup oil

½ cup water

4 eggs

6 small candy canes, crushed, divided

1 tub (8 oz.) COOL WHIP Whipped Topping, thawed

▸ make it!

HEAT oven to 350°F.

CHOP 4 oz. chocolate; set aside. Beat next 6 ingredients with mixer until well blended. Stir in chopped chocolate and 2 Tbsp. candy. Spoon into 30 paper-lined muffin cups.

BAKE 20 to 23 min. or until toothpick inserted into centers comes out clean. Cool in pans 10 min.; remove to wire racks. Cool completely.

MELT remaining 1 oz. chocolate; cool slightly. Frost cupcakes with COOL WHIP; drizzle with chocolate. Sprinkle with remaining candy.

spring fruit trifle

PREP: 15 min. | TOTAL: 45 min. | MAKES: 15 servings, ⅔ cup each.

▶ what you need!

36 vanilla wafers

2 Tbsp. orange-flavored liqueur

3 cups mixed fresh fruit (blueberries, sliced kiwi, sliced strawberries)

2 pkg. (3.4 oz. each) JELL-O Vanilla Flavor Instant Pudding

3 cups cold milk

1½ pkg. (4 oz. each) BAKER'S White Chocolate (6 oz.), broken into pieces, melted, cooled slightly

1 tub (8 oz.) COOL WHIP Whipped Topping, thawed, divided

▶ make it!

BREAK wafers coarsely; place on bottom of 2½-qt. trifle dish. Drizzle with liqueur. Top with fruit.

BEAT dry pudding mixes and milk in medium bowl with whisk 2 min. Stir in chocolate and half the COOL WHIP. Top fruit with pudding mixture.

TOP with remaining COOL WHIP. Refrigerate 30 min.

starlight mint cake

PREP: 30 min. | TOTAL: 4 hours 10 min. | MAKES: 16 servings.

▸ what you need!

- 1 pkg. (2-layer size) white cake mix
- 1 cup boiling water
- 1 pkg. (3 oz.) JELL-O Cherry Flavor Gelatin
- 28 starlight mints, divided
- 3 oz. BAKER'S White Chocolate, melted
- 2 Tbsp. BREAKSTONE'S or KNUDSEN Sour Cream
- 2 drops red food coloring
- 2 cups thawed COOL WHIP Whipped Topping

▸ make it!

PREPARE cake batter and bake as directed on package for 2 (9-inch) round cake layers. Cool cakes in pans 15 min. Pierce cakes with large fork at ½-inch intervals. Add boiling water to dry gelatin mix; stir 2 min. until completely dissolved. Pour over cakes. Refrigerate 3 hours.

HEAT oven to 350°F. Reserve 5 mints for later use. Place 12 of the remaining mints, about 4 inches apart, on parchment paper-covered baking sheet. Bake 5 min. or until mints are melted and each spreads out to 1½- to 2-inch circle. Remove from oven; cool completely before removing from parchment paper. Meanwhile, repeat with remaining 11 mints.

BLEND 5 reserved mints in blender until finely crushed; place in small bowl. Stir in melted chocolate, sour cream and food coloring.

DIP bottom of 1 cake pan in warm water 10 sec.; unmold onto serving plate. Spread cake with chocolate mixture. Unmold second cake layer; place on first layer. Frost with COOL WHIP. Decorate with melted mints. Keep refrigerated.

festive yule log "cake"

PREP: 30 min. | TOTAL: 12 hours 30 min. | MAKES: 14 servings.

▸ what you need!

- 1 pkg. (4 oz.) BAKER'S Semi-Sweet Chocolate, melted, cooled slightly and divided
- 5 vanilla wafers
- 1 pkg. (8 oz.) PHILADELPHIA Cream Cheese, softened
- ¼ cup butter, softened
- 1½ cups powdered sugar
- 1 pkg. (3.4 oz.) JELL-O Vanilla Flavor Instant Pudding
- 1 cup cold milk
- 1½ cups thawed COOL WHIP Whipped Topping
- 14 graham crackers, broken in half (28 squares)
- 1 oz. BAKER'S White Chocolate
- ¼ cup fresh raspberries

▸ make it!

PIPE small amount of semi-sweet chocolate into spiral design on wafers; refrigerate until ready to use. Beat cream cheese and butter in large bowl with mixer until well blended. Add remaining melted chocolate; mix well. Gradually beat in sugar until light and fluffy.

BEAT dry pudding mix and milk in medium bowl with whisk 2 min. Stir in COOL WHIP. Spread 1 rounded Tbsp. pudding mixture onto 1 graham square; cover with second graham square. Spread top with 1 rounded Tbsp. pudding mixture. Repeat with remaining graham squares and pudding mixture to form 12-inch loaf. Stand on edge of platter; frost with cream cheese mixture to resemble log.

RUN tines of fork over dessert to resemble tree bark. Refrigerate overnight. Meanwhile, make curls from white chocolate; refrigerate until ready to use. Decorate with wafers, chocolate curls and raspberries. Cut into diagonal slices to serve.

red and green holiday mold

PREP: 20 min. | TOTAL: 5 hours 20 min. | MAKES: 10 servings, ½ cup each.

▶ what you need!

2½ cups boiling water, divided

1 pkg. (6 oz.) JELL-O Gelatin, any red flavor

1 cup cold water

1 pkg. (3 oz.) JELL-O Lime Flavor Gelatin

1 cup vanilla ice cream, softened

½ cup thawed COOL WHIP Whipped Topping

▶ make it!

ADD 1½ cups boiling water to dry red gelatin mix in large bowl; stir 2 min. until completely dissolved. Stir in cold water. Reserve 1½ cups gelatin; let stand at room temperature. Pour remaining gelatin into 5-cup mold sprayed with cooking spray. Refrigerate 45 min. or until set but not firm.

STIR remaining boiling water into dry lime gelatin mix in medium bowl 2 min. until completely dissolved. Add ice cream; stir until completely melted. Spoon over red gelatin layer in mold. Refrigerate 20 min. or until gelatin is set but not firm.

SPOON reserved red gelatin over creamy layer in mold. Refrigerate 4 hours or until firm. Unmold. Top with COOL WHIP.

red, white & blueberry parfaits

PREP: 15 min. | TOTAL: 4 hours 15 min. | MAKES: 8 servings.

▶ what you need!

1 cup boiling water

1 pkg (0.6 oz.) JELL-O Strawberry Flavor Sugar Free Gelatin, or any other red flavor

1 cup cold water

1 tub (8 oz.) COOL WHIP FREE Whipped Topping, thawed, divided

1½ cups blueberries

▶ make it!

ADD boiling water to dry gelatin mix in medium bowl; stir 2 min. until completely dissolved. Stir in cold water. Pour into 13×9-inch pan.

REFRIGERATE 4 hours or until firm.

CUT gelatin into ½-inch cubes. Reserve 1 cup COOL WHIP for garnish. Layer blueberries, remaining COOL WHIP and gelatin in 8 dessert glasses. Top with reserved COOL WHIP.

patriotic gelatin in a cloud

PREP: 20 min. | TOTAL: 4 hours 20 min. | MAKES: 8 servings.

▸ what you need!

- 2 cups boiling water, divided
- 1 pkg. (3 oz.) JELL-O Strawberry Flavor Gelatin
- 1 pkg. (3 oz.) JELL-O Berry Blue Flavor Gelatin
- 1 cup cold water, divided
- 2 cups thawed COOL WHIP Whipped Topping

▸ make it!

STIR 1 cup of the boiling water into each flavor dry gelatin mix in separate medium bowls at least 2 min. until completely dissolved. Stir ½ cup of the cold water into gelatin in each bowl. Pour each flavor gelatin into separate 8-inch square pans. Refrigerate 4 hours or until firm.

DIP pans in warm water 15 sec. Cut gelatin into cubes, using sharp knife dipped in hot water. Loosen cubes from pan with spatula; refrigerate until ready to serve.

SPOON ¼ cup COOL WHIP into each of 8 dessert dishes just before serving. Using back of spoon, spread COOL WHIP onto bottom and up sides of each dish. Fill evenly with equal measures of the red and blue gelatin cubes. Store leftover desserts in refrigerator.

fourth of july party trifle

PREP: 20 min. | TOTAL: 4 hours 20 min. | MAKES: 18 servings, ⅔ cup each.

► what you need!

1½ cups boiling water

2 pkg. (3 oz. each) JELL-O Berry Blue Flavor Gelatin

1½ cups cold water

1 pkg. (10.75 oz.) frozen prepared pound cake, thawed, cubed

1 tub (8 oz.) COOL WHIP Whipped Topping, thawed

2 cups halved fresh strawberries

► make it!

STIR boiling water into dry gelatin mixes in large bowl at least 2 min. until completely dissolved. Stir in cold water. Pour into 13×9-inch pan. Refrigerate 3 hours or until firm.

CUT gelatin into ½-inch cubes. Place in 3½-qt. serving bowl. Cover with cake cubes, half of the COOL WHIP and the strawberries. Top with remaining COOL WHIP.

REFRIGERATE at least 1 hour before serving. Store leftovers in refrigerator.

merry cherry dessert

PREP: 20 min. | TOTAL: 3 hours 50 min. | MAKES: 18 servings, ⅔ cup each.

▸ what you need!

    1 can (21 oz.) cherry pie filling, divided

1½ cups boiling water

    1 pkg. (6 oz.) JELL-O Cherry Flavor Gelatin

1½ cups cold water

    4 cups angel food cake cubes

    2 pkg. (3.4 oz. each) JELL-O Vanilla Flavor Instant Pudding

    3 cups cold milk

    1 tub (8 oz.) COOL WHIP Whipped Topping, thawed, divided

▸ make it!

RESERVE ⅓ cup cherry pie filling for garnish; set aside. Add boiling water to dry gelatin mix in large bowl; stir at least 2 min. until completely dissolved. Stir in cold water and remaining cherry pie filling. Refrigerate 45 min. or until slightly thickened.

PLACE cake cubes in 3-qt. serving bowl; cover with gelatin mixture. Refrigerate 45 min. or until gelatin layer is set but not firm.

BEAT dry pudding mixes and milk in large bowl with whisk 2 min. Stir in 2 cups COOL WHIP; spoon over gelatin layer in bowl. Refrigerate 2 hours or until firm. Top with remaining COOL WHIP and reserved cherry pie filling.

holiday poke cake

PREP: 15 min. | TOTAL: 4 hours 30 min. | MAKES: 16 servings.

▶ what you need!

2 baked 9-inch round white cake layers, cooled

2 cups boiling water, divided

1 pkg. (3 oz.) JELL-O Gelatin, any red flavor

1 pkg. (3 oz.) JELL-O Lime Flavor Gelatin

1 tub (8 oz.) COOL WHIP Whipped Topping, thawed

¼ cup fresh raspberries

▶ make it!

PLACE cakes, top sides up, in clean 9-inch round cake pans; pierce with large fork at ½-inch intervals.

ADD 1 cup boiling water to each flavor dry gelatin mix in separate small bowls; stir 2 min. until completely dissolved. Pour red gelatin over 1 cake and lime gelatin over remaining cake. Refrigerate 3 hours.

DIP bottoms of cake pans in warm water 10 sec.; unmold. Fill and frost cake layers with COOL WHIP. Refrigerate 1 hour. Top with berries.

JELL-O firecrackers

PREP: 45 min. | TOTAL: 2 hours 45 min. | MAKES: 20 servings.

▶ what you need!

1⅓ cups boiling water, divided

1 pkg. (3 oz.) JELL-O Berry Blue Flavor Gelatin

1 pkg. (3 oz.) JELL-O Cherry Flavor Gelatin

1 env. KNOX* Unflavored Gelatine

1 cup milk, divided

3 Tbsp. sugar

½ tsp. vanilla

20 maraschino cherries with stems, well drained, patted dry

▶ make it!

ADD ⅔ cup boiling water to dry blue gelatin mix in small bowl; stir 2 min. until completely dissolved. Repeat with cherry gelatin mix. Cool.

MEANWHILE, sprinkle unflavored gelatine over ¼ cup milk in medium bowl; let stand 5 min. Bring remaining milk to boil in saucepan. Remove from heat; stir in sugar and vanilla. Add to plain gelatine mixture; stir until gelatine is completely dissolved. Cool 10 min.

SPOON blue gelatin into 20 (1-oz.) plastic shot glasses sprayed lightly with cooking spray, adding about 2 tsp. to each. Refrigerate 15 min. or until set but not firm.

TOP with unflavored gelatine mixture, adding about 2 tsp. to each cup. Refrigerate 10 min. Insert cherry, stem end up, into white gelatine layer in each cup. Refrigerate 2 min.

COVER with cherry gelatin, adding about 2 tsp. to each cup. Refrigerate 2 hours or until firm. Remove from cups before serving.

ADULTS ONLY ALCOHOLIC VARIATION:
Prepare as directed, reducing the boiling water to 1 cup and dissolving each of the berry and cherry gelatin mixes in ½ cup boiling water. Stir ¼ cup vodka into each flavor of gelatin, then continue as directed.

SUBSTITUTE:
Substitute blueberries and/or small strawberries for the cherries.

ADULTS ONLY SPIKED CHERRIES:
Place cherries in a glass jar. Add ½ cup vodka; cover with a tight-fitting lid. Refrigerate at least 2 hours; drain. Pat dry, then use as directed.

KNOX is a registered trademark of Kraft Foods Global, Inc.

chocolate elf bites

PREP: 15 min. | TOTAL: 2 hours 15 min. | MAKES: 18 servings.

▶ what you need!

1 pkg. (4 oz.) BAKER'S White Chocolate

½ cup butter or margarine, divided

⅓ cup water

1 pkg. (3.9 oz.) JELL-O Pistachio Flavor Instant Pudding

3 cups powdered sugar

2 oz. BAKER'S Semi-Sweet Chocolate

2 Tbsp. chopped pistachios

▶ make it!

LINE 8-inch square pan with foil, with ends of foil extending over sides. Microwave white chocolate, 6 Tbsp. butter and water in large microwaveable bowl on HIGH 2 min. or until butter is melted; stir with whisk until chocolate is completely melted and mixture is well blended.

ADD dry pudding mix; stir 2 min. Add sugar, 1 cup at a time, stirring after each addition until well blended. Press onto bottom of prepared pan.

MICROWAVE semi-sweet chocolate and remaining butter in large microwaveable bowl 1½ min. or until butter is melted. Stir until chocolate is completely melted and mixture is well blended; spread over fudge layer in pan. Sprinkle with nuts. Refrigerate 2 hours or until firm before cutting into 36 squares.

CHOCOLATE-BANANA FUDGE:
Prepare as directed, using JELL-O Banana Cream Flavor Instant Pudding and substituting chopped banana chips for the pistachios.

STORAGE KNOW-HOW:
Store cut-up fudge between sheets of waxed paper in airtight container in refrigerator up to 2 weeks.

monster shortbread cookies

PREP: 15 min. | TOTAL: 28 min. | MAKES: 15 servings.

▶ what you need!

      1 cup margarine or butter, softened

   1¼ cups all-purpose flour

    ¾ cup whole wheat flour

      1 pkg. (3 oz.) JELL-O Lime Flavor Gelatin

    15 maraschino cherries, well drained and halved, or 30 gummy cherry candies

▶ make it!

BEAT margarine in large bowl until creamy. Add flours and dry gelatin mix; beat until blended.

ROLL dough into 30 (1-inch balls); shape each into toe-shaped piece. Place, 2 inches apart, on baking sheet. Flatten 1 end of each slightly; press cherry half or candy into flattened end for the toenail. Use sharp knife to make crosswise slits in top of each toe for the knuckles.

BAKE 11 to 13 min. or until edges are lightly browned. Cool on baking sheet 5 min. Remove to wire racks; cool completely.

SIZE-WISE:
Sweets can be part of a balanced diet but remember to keep tabs on portions.

VARIATION:
Prepare using JELL-O Berry Blue Flavor Gelatin, and substituting 30 PLANTERS Pecan Halves for the 15 cherries/candies.

choco-cherry bread

PREP: 20 min. | TOTAL: 2 hours 45 min. | MAKES: 18 servings.

▶ what you need!

6 Tbsp. butter or margarine, softened

1 pkg. (3.9 oz.) JELL-O Chocolate Instant Pudding, divided

2 loaves (1 lb. each) frozen bread dough, thawed

2 Tbsp. butter or margarine, melted

½ cup dried cherries

½ cup chopped PLANTERS Pecans

2 Tbsp. powdered sugar

▶ make it!

MIX 6 Tbsp. butter and 2 Tbsp. dry pudding mix until blended. Refrigerate until ready to use.

ROLL out 1 loaf of dough into 14×8-inch rectangle on work surface sprinkled with 1 Tbsp. dry pudding mix; brush with 1 Tbsp. melted butter. Sprinkle with ¼ cup <u>each</u> of the remaining dry pudding mix, cherries and nuts; roll up, starting at one long side. Place, seam-side down, on parchment-covered baking sheet. Repeat with remaining dough and toppings.

COVER with plastic wrap. Let rise in warm place 45 min. or until doubled in volume.

HEAT oven to 350°F. Discard plastic wrap from dough. Bake dough 20 to 25 min. or until golden brown. Cool on baking sheet 5 min.; remove to wire rack. Cool completely. Sprinkle with powdered sugar. Serve with chocolate-flavored butter.

merry crunchmix

PREP: 15 min. | TOTAL: 25 min. | MAKES: 18 servings, about ½ cup each.

▸ what you need!

7 cups popped popcorn

1 cup small pretzel twists

1 cup PLANTERS Cashews

¼ cup butter or margarine

3 Tbsp. light corn syrup

½ cup sugar

1 pkg. (3 oz.) JELL-O Black Cherry Flavor Gelatin

▸ make it!

HEAT oven to 300°F.

LINE 15×10×1-inch pan with foil or waxed paper. Combine popcorn, pretzels and nuts.

COOK butter and syrup in saucepan on low heat until butter is melted. Add sugar and dry gelatin mix; cook and stir 2 min. or until completely dissolved. Bring to boil on medium heat; simmer on low heat 5 min. Pour over popcorn mixture; toss to evenly coat. Add to prepared pan; use 2 forks to spread into even layer.

BAKE 10 min.; cool. Break into small pieces.

SUBSTITUTE:
Substitute PLANTERS Lightly Salted Dry Roasted Peanuts for the cashews.

SUBSTITUTE:
Prepare using your favorite flavor of JELL-O Gelatin.

winter berry chocolate tart

PREP: 30 min. | TOTAL: 2 hours 40 min. | MAKES: 12 servings.

▶ what you need!

24 chocolate sandwich cookies, finely crushed (about 2 cups)

3 Tbsp. butter or margarine, melted

1½ pkg. (4 oz. each) BAKER'S Semi-Sweet Chocolate (6 oz.), divided

1 pkg. (3.9 oz.) JELL-O Chocolate Instant Pudding

1 cup cold milk

1 tub (8 oz.) COOL WHIP Whipped Topping, thawed, divided

¼ cup seedless raspberry jam

1 oz. BAKER'S White Chocolate

12 fresh raspberries

▶ make it!

SPRAY 10-inch tart pan with removable bottom with cooking spray. Mix cookie crumbs and butter; press onto bottom and up side of prepared pan. Refrigerate until ready to use.

MELT 2 oz. semi-sweet chocolate as directed on package. Beat dry pudding mix and milk in medium bowl with whisk 2 min. (Pudding will be thick.) Stir in melted chocolate, then 1 cup COOL WHIP until blended. Pour into crust. Refrigerate 1½ hours.

MICROWAVE remaining semi-sweet chocolate and COOL WHIP in microwaveable bowl on HIGH 2 min., stirring after 2 min. Stir until chocolate is completely melted and mixture is well blended. Cool 10 min.

MICROWAVE jam in separate microwaveable bowl on HIGH 15 sec.; spread over pudding layer in crust. Cover with COOL WHIP mixture. Refrigerate 30 min.

REMOVE tart from side of pan. Melt white chocolate as directed on package; drizzle over tart. Garnish with berries.

VARIATION:
Prepare using seedless strawberry jam and substituting 6 halved fresh strawberries for the raspberries.

merry berry christmas bites

PREP: 20 min. | TOTAL: 1 hour 10 min. | MAKES: 36 servings.

▶ what you need!

3 pkg. (4 oz. each) BAKER'S Semi-Sweet Chocolate (12 oz.), broken into pieces

4 tsp. shortening

1 pkg. (3 oz.) JELL-O Raspberry Flavor Gelatin

1 can (14 oz.) sweetened condensed milk

¼ tsp. almond extract

2 pkg. (7 oz. each) BAKER'S ANGEL FLAKE Coconut

▶ make it!

LINE 8-inch square pan with foil, with ends of foil extending over sides; spray with cooking spray. Microwave chocolate and shortening in medium microwaveable bowl on HIGH 1½ min.; stir. Microwave 1 min.; stir until chocolate is completely melted and mixture is well blended. Spread half onto bottom of prepared pan. Refrigerate 10 min.

MIX dry gelatin mix, milk and extract in large bowl until blended. Stir in coconut until evenly coated; spoon over chocolate layer in pan. Press gently into chocolate layer.

POUR remaining chocolate mixture over coconut layer; spread to completely cover coconut. Refrigerate 30 min. or until firm. Use foil handles to lift candy from pan; remove foil before cutting candy into squares.

HOW TO CUT CANDIES:
Use sharp knife to cut candy into pieces, dipping knife in warm water after each cut.

VARIATION:
Omit shortening. Prepare candy using BAKER'S White Chocolate and JELL-O Lime Flavor Gelatin.

frozen treats

Frosty make-ahead delights that are ready when you are

frozen chocolate "soufflés"

PREP: 10 min. | TOTAL: 5 hours 10 min. | MAKES: 8 servings, 1 "soufflé" each.

▶ what you need!

    3 cups milk

    2 pkg. (3.9 oz. each) JELL-O Chocolate Instant Pudding

    2 cups thawed COOL WHIP Whipped Topping

   16 chocolate sandwich cookies, finely chopped (about 2 cups)

    8 maraschino cherries

▶ make it!

POUR milk into medium bowl. Add dry pudding mixes. Beat with wire whisk 2 min. Gently stir in COOL WHIP.

SPOON 2 Tbsp. chopped cookies into each of 8 (8- to 9-oz.) paper drinking cups. Cover evenly with half of the pudding mixture. Press gently with the back of a spoon to eliminate air pockets. Repeat layers. Cover with foil.

FREEZE 5 hours or until firm. Remove from freezer about 15 min. before serving. Let stand at room temperature to soften slightly. Peel away paper to unmold onto dessert plates. Top each with a cherry. Store leftovers in freezer.

chocolate chunk & marshmallow sundae

PREP: 10 min. | TOTAL: 4 hours 10 min. | MAKES: 12 servings.

▶ what you need

2 pkg. (3.9 oz. each) JELL-O Chocolate Instant Pudding

2 cups cold milk

1 tub (8 oz.) COOL WHIP Whipped Topping, thawed

1 cup JET-PUFFED Miniature Marshmallows

4 oz. BAKER'S Semi-Sweet Chocolate, coarsely chopped

2 cups sliced fresh strawberries

▶ make it

BEAT dry pudding mixes and milk in large bowl with whisk 2 min.

STIR in COOL WHIP, marshmallows and chocolate.

SPOON into 2-qt. freezer-safe container; cover.

FREEZE 4 hours or until firm. Scoop into dessert dishes; top with berries

SPECIAL EXTRA:
Add other toppings, such as sliced bananas, fresh raspberries, chopped fresh pineapple, KRAFT Caramel Bits, BAKER'S ANGEL FLAKE Coconut and/or PLANTERS Dry Roasted Peanuts.

rocket pops

PREP: 30 min. | TOTAL: 7 hours 30 min. | MAKES: 16 servings, 1 pop each.

▶ what you need!

1 pkg. (3 oz.) JELL-O Cherry Flavor Gelatin

1 cup sugar, divided

2 cups boiling water, divided

Ice cubes

2 cups cold water, divided

1 pkg. (3 oz.) JELL-O Berry Blue Flavor Gelatin

1 tub (8 oz.) COOL WHIP Whipped Topping, thawed

▶ make it!

COMBINE dry cherry gelatin mix and ½ cup of the sugar in medium bowl. Add 1 cup of the boiling water; stir at least 2 min. until completely dissolved. Add enough ice cubes to 1 cup of the cold water to measure 2 cups. Add to gelatin; stir until ice is completely melted. Pour evenly into 16 (5-oz.) paper or plastic cups, adding about ¼ cup of the gelatin to each cup. Freeze 1 hour.

MEANWHILE, combine dry blue gelatin mix and remaining ½ cup sugar in medium bowl. Add remaining 1 cup boiling water; stir at least 2 min. until completely dissolved. Add enough ice cubes to remaining 1 cup cold water to measure 2 cups. Add to gelatin; stir until ice is completely melted. Refrigerate 1 hour.

SPOON about 3 Tbsp. COOL WHIP over red gelatin in each cup; top evenly with blue gelatin, adding about ¼ cup of the gelatin to each cup. Freeze 1 hour or until almost firm. Insert wooden pop stick or plastic spoon into center of each cup for handle. Freeze an additional 4 hours or overnight. To remove pops from cups, place bottoms of cups under warm running water for 15 sec. Press firmly on bottoms of cups to release pops. (Do not twist or pull pop sticks.) Store leftover pops in freezer.

sparkling lemon ice

PREP: 20 min. | TOTAL: 3 hours 20 min. | MAKES: 6 servings.

▸ what you need!

- 1 cup boiling water
- 1 pkg. (0.3 oz.) JELL-O Lemon Flavor Sugar Free Gelatin
- 1 cup cold lemon lime-flavored seltzer
- ½ tsp. grated lemon zest
- 3 Tbsp. fresh lemon juice

▸ make it!

STIR boiling water into dry gelatin mix in medium bowl at least 2 min. until completely dissolved. Stir in remaining ingredients. Pour into 9-inch square pan; cover.

FREEZE 3 hours or until frozen.

REMOVE from freezer; let stand at room temperature 10 min. to soften slightly. Beat with electric mixer on high speed until smooth. Spoon into 6 dessert dishes to serve. Store leftovers in freezer.

strawberry snow cones

PREP: 10 min. | TOTAL: 10 min. | MAKES: 8 servings.

▸ what you need!

- 1 cup boiling water
- 1 pkg. (6 oz.) JELL-O Gelatin, any red flavor
- 1 cup puréed strawberries
- ½ cup light corn syrup
- ½ cup ice cubes
- 8 cups crushed ice

▸ make it!

ADD boiling water to dry gelatin mix in large bowl; stir 2 min. until completely dissolved. Add strawberries, corn syrup and ice cubes; stir until ice is completely melted.

SPOON crushed ice into 8 (8-oz.) paper or plastic cups.

SPOON gelatin mixture over ice. Serve immediately.

triple strawberry no-drip pops

PREP: 10 min. | TOTAL: 2 hours 10 min. | MAKES: 8 servings.

▸ what you need!

2 cups boiling water

1 pkg. (3 oz.) JELL-O Strawberry Flavor Gelatin

18 fresh strawberries, stemmed

⅔ cup (filled to 2-qt. line) KOOL-AID Strawberry Flavor Sugar-Sweetened Soft
Drink Mix, or any red flavor

▸ make it!

ADD boiling water to dry gelatin mix; stir 2 min. until completely dissolved.

CUT strawberries in half. Mash berries and drink mix in large bowl with fork. Stir in
gelatin.

POUR into 8 (5-oz.) paper cups.

COVER cups with foil, insert wooden pop stick into center of each for handle. Freeze
2 hours or until firm.

cupcakes, pops, & small bites

Tiny treats everyone will love

JELL-O pastel cookies

PREP: 30 min. | TOTAL: 40 min. | MAKES: about 5 dozen cookies or 30 servings, 2 cookies each.

▶ what you need!

3½ cups flour

1 tsp. CALUMET Baking Powder

1½ cups butter or margarine, softened

1 cup sugar

2 pkg. (3 oz. each) JELL-O Gelatin, any flavor, divided

1 egg

1 tsp. vanilla

▶ make it!

HEAT oven to 400°F.

MIX flour and baking powder; set aside. Beat butter in large bowl with mixer until creamy. Gradually add sugar and 1 pkg. gelatin; beat until light and fluffy. Blend in egg and vanilla. Gradually add flour mixture, beating well after each addition.

SHAPE dough into 1-inch balls. Place, 2 inches apart, on baking sheets. Flatten with bottom of glass. Sprinkle with remaining dry gelatin.

BAKE 8 to 10 min. or until edges are lightly browned. Let stand on baking sheets 3 min. Remove to wire racks. Cool completely.

JELL-O homemade pudding pops

PREP: 10 min. | TOTAL: 5 hours 10 min. | MAKES: 6 servings.

▶ what you need!

1 pkg. (3.9 oz.) JELL-O Chocolate Instant Pudding

2 cups cold milk

▶ make it!

BEAT ingredients with whisk 2 min.

POUR into 6 (5-oz.) paper or plastic cups. Insert wooden pop stick or plastic spoon into center of each cup.

FREEZE 5 hours or until firm. Peel off paper cups before serving.

wigglin' jigglin' cupcakes

PREP: 45 min. | TOTAL: 3 hours 45 min. | MAKES: 2 dozen or 24 servings, 1 cupcake each.

▶ what you need!

2½ cups boiling water (Do not add cold water.)

2 pkg. (3 oz. each) JELL-O Cherry Flavor Gelatin

1 pkg. (2-layer size) yellow cake mix

1 tub (8 oz.) COOL WHIP Whipped Topping, thawed

Colored sprinkles

▶ make it!

STIR boiling water into dry gelatin mixes in medium bowl at least 3 min. until completely dissolved. Pour into 15×10×1-inch pan.

REFRIGERATE at least 3 hours or until firm. Meanwhile, prepare and bake cake mix as directed on package for 24 cupcakes. Cool completely on wire racks. Cut each cupcake in half horizontally.

DIP bottom of 15×10×1-inch pan in warm water about 15 sec. Using 2-inch round cookie cutter, cut out 24 JIGGLERS. Place a small dollop of COOL WHIP on bottom half of each cupcake; top with JIGGLERS circle and another small dollop of COOL WHIP. Place top half of cupcake on each stack; press gently into COOL WHIP. Top with the remaining COOL WHIP and sprinkles.

chocolate-peanut butter cupcakes

PREP: 20 min. | TOTAL: 1 hour 20 min. | MAKES: 24 servings.

▶ what you need!

1 pkg. (2-layer size) devil's food cake mix

1 pkg. (3.4 oz.) JELL-O Vanilla Flavor Instant Pudding

1 cup cold milk

½ cup PLANTERS Creamy Peanut Butter

1½ cups thawed COOL WHIP Whipped Topping

1 pkg. (4 oz.) BAKER'S Semi-Sweet Chocolate

¼ cup PLANTERS Dry Roasted Peanuts, chopped

▶ make it!

HEAT oven to 350°F.

PREPARE cake batter and bake in 24 paper-lined muffin cups as directed on package. Cool 30 min. (Cupcakes need to still be warm to fill.)

BEAT dry pudding mix and milk with whisk 2 min. Add peanut butter; mix well. Spoon into small freezer-weight resealable plastic bag; seal bag. Snip off one corner from bottom of bag. Insert tip of bag into center of each cupcake; pipe in about 1 Tbsp. filling.

MICROWAVE COOL WHIP and chocolate in microwaveable bowl on HIGH 1½ min. or until chocolate is completely melted and mixture is well blended, stirring after 1 min. Dip tops of cupcakes into glaze. Sprinkle with nuts.

holiday poke cupcakes

PREP: 30 min. | TOTAL: 1 hour | MAKES: 24 servings.

▶ what you need!

1 pkg. (2-layer size) white cake mix

1 cup boiling water

1 pkg. (3 oz.) JELL-O Gelatin, any red flavor

1 tub (8 oz.) COOL WHIP Whipped Topping, thawed

Red or green food coloring (optional)

Decorations: colored sugar, colored sprinkles, crushed candy canes and/or JET-PUFFED HOLIDAY MALLOWS Marshmallows

▶ make it!

PREPARE cake batter and bake as directed on package for 24 cupcakes. Cool in pans 10 min. (Do not remove from pans.) Pierce tops with fork.

ADD boiling water to dry gelatin mix; stir 2 min. until completely dissolved. Spoon over cupcakes. Refrigerate 30 min. Remove from pans.

TINT COOL WHIP with food coloring, if desired; spread COOL WHIP onto cupcakes. Decorate as desired.

JELL-O mini trifle bites

PREP: 10 min. | TOTAL: 2 hours 10 min. | MAKES: 12 servings.

▶ what you need!

2 cups boiling water

2 pkg. (0.3 oz. each) JELL-O Raspberry Flavor Sugar Free Gelatin

3 slices fat-free pound cake (¾-inch-thick), cut into 24 cubes

1 pkg. (8 oz.) PHILADELPHIA Neufchâtel Cheese, softened

1 cup powdered sugar

1 cup thawed COOL WHIP LITE Whipped Topping

1 tsp. lemon zest

▶ make it!

ADD boiling water to dry gelatin mixes in large bowl; stir 2 min. or until completely dissolved. Place 1 cake cube in each of 24 mini muffin cups lined with paper or foil liners; cover with gelatin. Refrigerate 2 hours or until firm.

BEAT Neufchâtel in small bowl with mixer until creamy. Gradually beat in sugar. Gently stir in COOL WHIP and zest.

SPOON into pastry bag fitted with star tip. Use to pipe Neufchâtel mixture over trifles.

firecracker bites

PREP: 40 min. | TOTAL: 2 hours 30 min. | MAKES: 14 servings, 3 wafer sandwiches each.

▶ what you need!

  1 pkg. (8 oz.) PHILADELPHIA Cream Cheese, softened

  1 cup cold milk

  1 pkg. (3.4 oz.) JELL-O Vanilla Flavor Instant Pudding

  1½ cups thawed COOL WHIP Whipped Topping, divided

  1 pkg. (12 oz.) vanilla wafers

  ½ cup mixed red, white and blue sprinkles

  42 pieces red string licorice (1 inch)

▶ make it!

BEAT cream cheese in large bowl with mixer until creamy. Gradually beat in milk. Add dry pudding mix; beat 2 min. Whisk in 1 cup COOL WHIP.

SPOON about 1½ Tbsp. pudding mixture onto each of half the wafers; cover with remaining wafers to make sandwiches. Freeze 2 hours or until filling is firm.

SPREAD tops of wafer sandwiches with remaining COOL WHIP. Dip in sprinkles. Insert licorice piece into top of each for the fuse. Freeze until ready to serve.

pineapple upside-down cupcakes

PREP: 20 min. | TOTAL: 38 min. | MAKES: 24 servings.

▶ what you need

½ cup packed brown sugar

¼ cup butter, melted

2 cans (8 oz. each) pineapple tidbits in juice, drained

½ cup chopped PLANTERS Pecans

12 maraschino cherries, halved

1 cup boiling water

1 pkg. (3 oz.) JELL-O Lemon Flavor Gelatin

1 pkg. (2-layer size) yellow cake mix

4 eggs

⅔ cup oil

2 tsp. lemon zest

▶ make it

HEAT oven to 350°F.

MIX sugar and butter in medium bowl; stir in pineapple and nuts. Place cherry half, cut-side up, in center of each of 24 paper-lined muffin cups. Cover with pineapple mixture.

ADD boiling water to dry gelatin mix; stir 2 min. until completely dissolved. Cool 10 min.

BEAT remaining ingredients in large bowl with mixer until well blended. Add gelatin; mix well. Spoon over pineapple mixture in muffin cups. (Cups will almost be completely filled.)

BAKE 15 to 18 min. or until toothpick inserted in centers comes out clean. Cool in pans 10 min.; remove from pans to wire racks. Cool completely. Invert onto plates just before serving; remove paper liners.

black forest cupcakes

PREP: 20 min. | TOTAL: 1 hour 2 min. | MAKES: 24 servings.

▶ what you need!

1 pkg. (2-layer size) chocolate cake mix

½ cup boiling water

1 pkg. (3 oz.) JELL-O Black Cherry Flavor Gelatin

1½ cups thawed COOL WHIP Whipped Topping

24 maraschino cherries with stems, drained

▶ make it!

PREPARE cake batter and bake as directed on package for 24 cupcakes; cool completely.

ADD boiling water to dry gelatin mix in medium bowl; stir 2 min. until completely dissolved. Refrigerate 15 min. or until slightly thickened.

WHISK COOL WHIP gradually into gelatin until well blended. Spread onto cupcakes, using about 2 Tbsp. for each. Top with cherries just before serving.

ORANGE CREAM CUPCAKES:
Prepare using a yellow cake mix and JELL-O Orange Flavor Gelatin. Substitute twisted orange slices for the cherries.

HOW TO STORE:
Keep refrigerated.

VARIATION:
Prepare using 1 pkg. (0.3 oz.) JELL-O Black Cherry Flavor Sugar Free Gelatin and COOL WHIP LITE Whipped Topping.

layered lemon-grape bites

PREP: 15 min. | TOTAL: 1 hour 15 min. | MAKES: 32 servings.

▸ what you need!

1½ cups boiling water, divided

3 pkg. (3 oz. each) JELL-O Lemon Flavor Gelatin, divided

⅔ cup seedless red grapes, quartered

⅔ cup seedless green grapes, quartered

½ cup BREAKSTONE'S or KNUDSEN Sour Cream

▸ make it!

ADD ½ cup boiling water to 1 pkg. dry gelatin mix; stir 2 min. until completely dissolved. Pour into 9-inch square pan sprayed with cooking spray; top with grapes. Refrigerate 20 min. or until gelatin is set but not firm.

MEANWHILE, add remaining boiling water to remaining gelatin mixes; stir 2 min. until completely dissolved. Let stand at room temperature until ready to use.

WHISK sour cream into cooled gelatin in bowl until blended; pour over gelatin in pan. Refrigerate 1 hour or until firm. Unmold before cutting to serve.

SPECIAL EXTRA:
Garnish with frosted grapes just before serving. Dip 32 additional seedless grapes in lemon juice, then roll in ¼ cup sugar. Gently shake grapes to remove excess sugar before using to garnish dessert. Discard remaining sugar.

FOOD FACTS:
You will need about 15 grapes to yield ⅔ cup.

reduced sugar strawberry-yogurt bites

PREP: 10 min. | TOTAL: 3 hours 10 min. | MAKES: 16 servings.

▶ what you need!

3 containers (6 oz. each) strawberry light nonfat yogurt

1 pkg. (0.3 oz.) JELL-O Strawberry Flavor Sugar Free Gelatin

8 fresh strawberries, halved

▶ make it!

MIX yogurt and dry gelatin mix in 1½-qt. microwaveable bowl. Microwave on HIGH 2 min.; stir. Microwave 2 to 3 min. or until completely dissolved, stirring after each minute.

SPOON into 16 paper-lined mini muffin pan cups. Refrigerate 1 hour or until firm.

REMOVE yogurt bites from liners; top with strawberries.

index

METRIC CONVERSION CHART

VOLUME MEASUREMENTS (dry)

$\frac{1}{8}$ teaspoon = 0.5 mL
$\frac{1}{4}$ teaspoon = 1 mL
$\frac{1}{2}$ teaspoon = 2 mL
$\frac{3}{4}$ teaspoon = 4 mL
1 teaspoon = 5 mL
1 tablespoon = 15 mL
2 tablespoons = 30 mL
$\frac{1}{4}$ cup = 60 mL
$\frac{1}{3}$ cup = 75 mL
$\frac{1}{2}$ cup = 125 mL
$\frac{2}{3}$ cup = 150 mL
$\frac{3}{4}$ cup = 175 mL
1 cup = 250 mL
2 cups = 1 pint = 500 mL
3 cups = 750 mL
4 cups = 1 quart = 1 L

VOLUME MEASUREMENTS (fluid)

1 fluid ounce (2 tablespoons) = 30 mL
4 fluid ounces ($\frac{1}{2}$ cup) = 125 mL
8 fluid ounces (1 cup) = 250 mL
12 fluid ounces (1$\frac{1}{2}$ cups) = 375 mL
16 fluid ounces (2 cups) = 500 mL

WEIGHTS (mass)

$\frac{1}{2}$ ounce = 15 g
1 ounce = 30 g
3 ounces = 90 g
4 ounces = 120 g
8 ounces = 225 g
10 ounces = 285 g
12 ounces = 360 g
16 ounces = 1 pound = 450 g

DIMENSIONS

$\frac{1}{16}$ inch = 2 mm
$\frac{1}{8}$ inch = 3 mm
$\frac{1}{4}$ inch = 6 mm
$\frac{1}{2}$ inch = 1.5 cm
$\frac{3}{4}$ inch = 2 cm
1 inch = 2.5 cm

OVEN TEMPERATURES

250°F = 120°C
275°F = 140°C
300°F = 150°C
325°F = 160°C
350°F = 180°C
375°F = 190°C
400°F = 200°C
425°F = 220°C
450°F = 230°C

BAKING PAN SIZES

Utensil	Size in Inches/Quarts	Metric Volume	Size in Centimeters
Baking or Cake Pan (square or rectangular)	8×8×2	2 L	20×20×5
	9×9×2	2.5 L	23×23×5
	12×8×2	3 L	30×20×5
	13×9×2	3.5 L	33×23×5
Loaf Pan	8×4×3	1.5 L	20×10×7
	9×5×3	2 L	23×13×7
Round Layer Cake Pan	8×1½	1.2 L	20×4
	9×1½	1.5 L	23×4
Pie Plate	8×1¼	750 mL	20×3
	9×1¼	1 L	23×3
Baking Dish or Casserole	1 quart	1 L	—
	1½ quarts	1.5 L	—
	2 quarts	2 L	—